I Will Not Be Bullied, I Will Not Bully Others

Marie C. Zoutomou- Quintanilla

WestBow Press books may be ordered through booksellers or by contacting:

WestBow Press
A Division of Thomas Nelson & Zondervan
1663 Liberty Drive
Bloomington, IN 47403
www.westbowpress.com
1 (866) 928-1240

Because of the dynamic nature of the Internet, any web addresses or links contained in this book may have changed since publication and may no longer be valid. The views expressed in this work are solely those of the author and do not necessarily reflect the views of the publisher, and the publisher hereby disclaims any responsibility for them.

This book is a work of non-fiction. Unless otherwise noted, the author and the publisher make no explicit guarantees as to the accuracy of the information contained in this book and in some cases, names of people and places have been altered to protect their privacy.

Any people depicted in stock imagery provided by Getty Images are models, and such images are being used for illustrative purposes only. Certain stock imagery © Getty Images.

ISBN: 978-1-9736-3990-9 (sc)
ISBN: 978-1-9736-3991-6 (e)

Library of Congress Control Number: 2018910986

Print information available on the last page.

WestBow Press rev. date: 11/13/2018

WESTBOW
PRESS®
A DIVISION OF THOMAS NELSON
& ZONDERVAN

I Will Not Be Bullied, I Will Not Bully Others

I WILL NOT BE BULLIED
My mommy loves me
My daddy loves me
I WILL NOT BE BULLIED

I stand strong and with confidence

I feel self-assured and believe in my own abilities

"I trust myself."

"I have faith in myself."

"I believe in myself."

INSTA TOON

You stand strong and with confidence
I WILL NOT BULLY OTHERS
Your mommy loves you
Your daddy loves you
I WILL NOT BULLY OTHERS

Stand Strong: When I think I may give in I tell myself, "I can do it, and I **got** this."

I WILL NOT BE BULLIED
My mommy loves me
My daddy loves me
I WILL NOT BE BULLIED

I walk with my head up high and shoulders back

"I learned to walk."

"I learned to brush my own teeth."

"I learned to ride my bike."

You walk with your head up high and shoulders back
I WILL NOT BULLY OTHERS
Your mommy loves you
Your daddy loves you
I WILL NOT BULLY OTHERS

Head up high and shoulders back, I achieve something every day.

I WILL NOT BE BULLIED
My mommy loves me
My daddy loves me
I WILL NOT BE BULLIED

I talk with a clear and firm voice

"I slow down when I am talking."

"I speak with a relaxed tone."

"I watch my body language."

You talk with a clear and firm voice
I WILL NOT BULLY OTHERS
Your mommy loves you
Your daddy loves you
I WILL NOT BULLY OTHERS

Clear and firm voice: the message I want to send
is supported by my tone and posture.

I WILL NOT BE BULLIED
My mommy loves me
My daddy loves me
I WILL NOT BE BULLIED

I look into people's eyes when talking to them

"I look at people when I talk and
when they talk to me."

"I practice eye contact with mommy
and daddy at home."

"I hold my eye contact."

You look into people's eyes when you talk to them
I WILL NOT BULLY OTHERS
Your mommy loves you
Your daddy loves you
I WILL NOT BULLY OTHERS

I respect other people and always look them in the eyes. One of the easiest ways to tell them what I mean is looking them square in the face!

I WILL NOT BE BULLIED
My mommy loves me
My daddy loves me
I WILL NOT BE BULLIED

**Mommy and daddy play with me and
we enjoy spending time together**

"Sometimes mommy and daddy direct
playtime, and sometimes I show
them how I want to play."

"We play pretend and sing songs, we
dance, play games, and read together."

"We play outdoors as well!"

Your mommy and daddy play with you and you enjoy spending time with them
I WILL NOT BULLY OTHERS
Your mommy loves you
Your daddy loves you
I WILL NOT BULLY OTHERS

Playing together helps me learn and bond with mommy and daddy.

My cousins play with me, too!

I WILL NOT BE BULLIED
My mommy loves me
My daddy loves me
I WILL NOT BE BULLIED

I say my feelings, loud and clear

"I listen to my feelings when talking."

"I listen to others' feelings when
they're talking to me."

"It is important to say my feelings,
good or bad, constructively."

You say your feelings, loud and clear
I WILL NOT BULLY OTHERS
Your mommy loves you
Your daddy loves you
I WILL NOT BULLY OTHERS

Say my feelings: saying how I feel will help me feel better on the inside.

I WILL NOT BE BULLIED
My mommy loves me
My daddy loves me
I WILL NOT BE BULLIED

My mommy and daddy are my first heroes

"Mommy and Daddy love me."

"Mommy and Daddy take good care of me."

"Mommy and Daddy teach me
new things every day."

Your mommy and daddy are your first heroes
I WILL NOT BULLY OTHERS
Your mommy loves you
Your daddy loves you
I WILL NOT BULLY OTHERS

My heroes

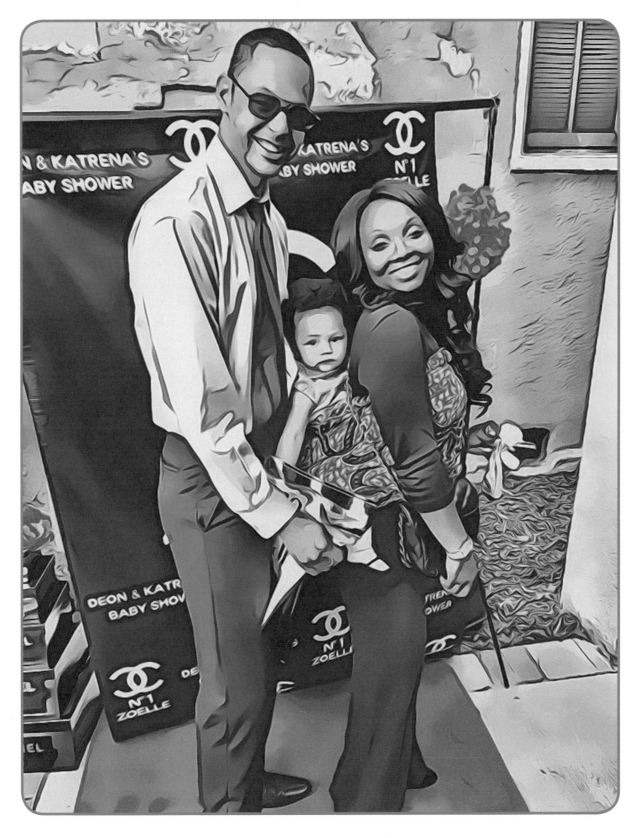

WE WILL NOT BE BULLIED
Our mommies love us
Our daddies love us
WE WILL NOT BE BULLIED

'No one has the right to bully me.

I stand strong and with
confidence and let them see

I'm shielded by love, from
those near to my heart,

And the angels up above.'

WE WILL NOT BULLY OTHERS
Your mommy loves you
Your daddy loves you
WE WILL NOT BULLY OTHERS

Daily affirmations

(Say it 1 time before going to school in the morning and 1 time before going to bed.)

1) I stand strong and with confidence
2) I walk with my head up high and shoulders back
3) I talk with a clear and firm voice
4) I look into people's eyes when talking to them
5) Mommy and daddy play with me and we enjoy spending time together
6) I say my feelings, loud and clear
7) My mommy and daddy are my heroes

Mommy and daddy love us!

THE END

One thing that mom and dad (Marie Zoutomou-Quintanilla and Jayson Quintanilla) want is a confident kid. We wanted to share our perspective on how to instill self-confidence into any child. Self-confidence is a critical part of life and influences areas such as education, career choice, self-fulfillment, relationships, and independent, critical thinking.

I WILL NOT BE BULLIED, I WILL NOT BULLY OTHERS

is a series of books to help our children to gain self-confidence as they transition from childhood to the teenage years and finally, adulthood. These books are written by a mom who is an author/motivational speaker and a dad who has been a teacher for 17 years.

This 5-book series follows the growing process of our child from infancy to 8 years old, 9-12 years old, the teenage years, and adulthood.

Email: thetestbymarie@yahoo.com

Website: iwillnotbebulliediwillnotbullyothers.com

Schools, Libraries, Learning Centers, Daycares and Churches can book us to do 20min to 30min training classes on self-confidence.

Facebook: https://www.facebook.com/youarebeingtested/